Once Upon A Dream

Imagine

Edited By Debbie Killingworth

First published in Great Britain in 2024 by:

YoungWriters Est. 1991

Young Writers
Remus House
Coltsfoot Drive
Peterborough
PE2 9BF
Telephone: 01733 890066
Website: www.youngwriters.co.uk

All Rights Reserved
Book Design by Ashley Janson
© Copyright Contributors 2024
Softback ISBN 978-1-83565-914-4
Printed and bound in the UK by BookPrintingUK
Website: www.bookprintinguk.com
YB0611F

FOREWORD

Welcome Reader, to a world of dreams.

For Young Writers' latest competition, we asked our writers to dig deep into their imagination and create a poem that paints a picture of what they dream of, whether it's a make-believe world full of wonder or their aspirations for the future.

The result is this collection of fantastic poetic verse that covers a whole host of different topics. Let your mind fly away with the fairies to explore the sweet joy of candy lands, join in with a game of fantasy football, or you may even catch a glimpse of a unicorn or another mythical creature. Beware though, because even dreamland has dark corners, so you may turn a page and walk into a nightmare!

Whereas the majority of our writers chose to stick to a free verse style, others gave themselves the challenge of other techniques such as acrostics and rhyming couplets. We also gave the writers the option to compose their ideas in a story, so watch out for those narrative pieces too!

Each piece in this collection shows the writers' dedication and imagination – we truly believe that seeing their work in print gives them a well-deserved boost of pride, and inspires them to keep writing, so we hope to see more of their work in the future!

CONTENTS

Bellyeoman Primary School, Dunfermline

Freya Candlish (11)	1
Rachel Cockburn (11)	2
Ava Peddie (10)	4
Layla Duthie (10)	6
Zuzanna Gajda (11)	8
Molly Walker (11)	9
Olivia Rodrigues Teixeira (10)	10
Jessica Cronin (11)	12
Oliver Platten (10)	13
Euan Simmonette (10)	14
Ram Leanillo (10)	15
Jackson Russell (10)	16
Conrad Abraham (12)	17
Lewis Thompson (10)	18
Jay Brownlie (10)	19
Alice Nicholson (10)	20
Ruby Popescu (10)	21
Neve Smith (11)	22
Ella Reid (10)	23
Brogan Lamb (10)	24
Isaac McKenzie (10)	25

Bracoden School, Gamrie

Leela Walker (9)	26
Logan McLean (10)	27
Scott Ritchie (9)	28

Chigwell Primary Academy, Chigwell

Freddie Folan (10)	29
Nelson Landing Flanagan (10)	30

Humaira Islam (10)	32
Toluwanimi Adeyinka (9)	33
Olly Wymer (10)	34
Talia Gadiagellan (10)	35
Nilisha Vimaleswaran (10)	36
Lenny Wren	37
Shray Vekariya (10)	38
Clark Harman (11)	39

Larbert Village Primary School, Larbert

Zoe Cartwright (9)	40
Sophia Ure (9)	42
Jessica Thom (10)	43
Oliver Smart (9)	44
Aaron Auchinvole (9)	45
Sasha Wylie (9)	46
Emily Maclean (9)	47
Katie Taylor (9)	48
Lottie Wilson (9)	49
Jasper Switzer (10)	50
Ruby Lyon (10)	51
Ryan Wilson (9)	52
Millie Nicolson (9)	53
Fraser Wallace (9)	54
Leah Barrowman (9)	55
Connor Newlands (10)	56
Ralph Walker (9)	57
Murron Pettigrew (10)	58

Lorne Primary School, Edinburgh

Archie Moore (9)	59
Makarios Yerikema (9)	60
Allan Nuñez (9)	62

Nora Salgado-Cerezo (9)	63
Lewis Burnett (9)	64
Elliot Laidlaw (8)	65
Mason Tipton (9)	66
Polina Kucher (9)	67
Afroze Faizan (9)	68
Taleen Ujam (8)	69
Cee Cee Mason (8)	70
Akorede Agunbiade (8)	71

Netherthird Primary School, Cumnock

Rhys Rinaldi (11)	72
Khloe Carmichael (11)	74
Darcie Reid (10)	75
Jorgie Hodge (11)	76
Caitlyn Williams (10)	77

St Sylvester's RC Primary School, Elgin

Joshua Powrie (10)	78
Blanca Mazela (11)	79
Zofia Andrasovska (11)	80
Alan Cetera (10)	81
Bladean Blantier (12)	82

Thornton Primary School, Thornton

Alana Graham (11)	83
Charlie M (11)	84
Grace Muldoon (10)	85
Lucy B (10)	86
Kerensa T-S (10)	87
Brianna T (11)	88
Jack P (10)	89
Adam H (11)	90
Casey M (10)	91
Mitchell A (11)	92
Dexter M (10)	93
Freddie Fox (10)	94
Caitlyn B (11)	95

Tyler T (10)	96
Poppy Donaldson (11)	97

West Coats Primary School, Cambuslang

Jenna Spy (10)	98
Arran Forbes (9)	100
Isla Fraser (10)	101
Julia Laing (9)	102
Eva McNab (9)	103
Callum Forrest (9)	104
Callum MacLeod (9)	105
Grace Shields (9)	106
Logan Thomas (10)	107
Erin Carr (10)	108
Lucy Woodcraft (9)	109
Mia Chow (10)	110
Scott Allen (9)	111
Millie Glover (9)	112
Finn Scott (10)	113
Orla Dyer (10)	114
Shanzay Zahid (10)	115
Cooper Scott (9)	116
Aaron Cole (9)	117
Theo Nicolson (9)	118
Daniel Butler (9)	119

Willoughby Primary School, Loughborough

Mabel Edwards (9)	120
Rae Tattersall (7)	121
Jessica White (10)	122
Isabelle Cook (9)	123

THE CREATIVE WRITING

The Fright

I was upside down in Dream Land...
The sky was as green as emeralds.
The floor was covered in clouds
And birds chirped at our feet.
My dog, Nellie was made of chocolate with candy cane bits as eyes
She was going to rise into the deep blue skies
And then she lay on a cloud as flat as a pancake hoping she could go buy a fat cake.
Then she saw a humongous chocolate river
That looked like a mud pile but was really chocolate.
Her biggest dream, a chocolate river she could eat too.

Nellie thought it was poisonous chocolate and she jumped in like a professional diver.
She heard the splash but she didn't realise that there were candy canes.
Nellie felt a bit like jelly but Nellie liked it.
Nellie started to fear but then it started to appear.
And the candy canes rose in the deep blue skies.
Nellie started to have fun then she was on the run
Because the clouds started to roar...
And that's the story of the fright.

Freya Candlish (11)
Bellyeoman Primary School, Dunfermline

Through A Magic Mirror

At 3 o'clock a mirror appeared between two pillars.
This could be someone's biggest fear as faces quickly started to appear.
I put my hand on the mirror, my hands fell through.
What could I do?
I walked through the mirror and thought it was a mistake but everything turned out to be great or so I thought...

Then I heard a shriek just then a girl appeared,
She was holding a doll that started to move.
I asked her where I was,
She said, "You'll see, just follow me."
The girl whispered a crazy spell,
I was scared as you could tell.
She said I was at the beginning but when I heard the singing,
The monsters and their creepiness would be like a distant ringing,
With a boom, bang, swirl and a spin,
Next I heard the ground start to sing.

A bright white light in my head,
I realised it was snow.
As tiny creatures are rowing on tiny boats,
massive birds in the sky holding little mini kites like a flag in the sky.
A little puppy came to my feet,
He had little horns on his head,
But he was like a little angel and then he ran away.
In the water I saw a fish, a rainbow fish,
Where I ended up was like my biggest wish.
Sweets filled the sky
And a half man, half horse said hello and told me it was time to go.

Before I leave I want you all to know, what it looks like,
This will be quite a show.
There was a little river with mirrors on either side of this luscious land.
The clouds were smiling but when it was a starry night the stars would smile and wave at you and someday you might see them too.

Rachel Cockburn (11)
Bellyeoman Primary School, Dunfermline

One Tick Till Goodbye

I'm lying in bed when a thought hits my head.
What happens when we can say that we are dead?
I sit up and look around, hear a slight ticking sound.

I get up out of bed to read a book instead.
The ticking gets louder, I look at my clock.
One tick till midnight.
No wonder I got such a shock.
Tick-tock!

All of a sudden, I screech in horror.
As the pages of my book grow taller and taller.
The minute hand starts to spin.
Making me screech and dragging me in.
Red devil eyes and a long scaly tail,
Making me scared, that can be fatal.

But just then I realise where I am.
Hell!
That's it,
Is this where I come when I must say goodbye?
"No!" says a voice from up really high.

I look up to see a bright white light,
White feathery wings pull me through the night.
I get dropped off in a warm fuzzy place.
Floor made of clouds, sky full of sun.
This place looks like lots of fun.

I meet a man with angel wings,
And thankfully it's good news he brings.
Golden rings he throws on the clouds
Opens a portal back to the ground.

And that's when I wake up.

Ava Peddie (10)
Bellyeoman Primary School, Dunfermline

The Wishing Star

Birds chirp at night and sleep during the day
People have midnight walks
No one knows why foxes and wolves come out during the day
Cats and dogs come out at night...
At night it is cold and quiet
Stars are light and purplish and pinkish...

Once upon a time, there was a little girl named Valeria
She was a sweetheart
She was bored of lying in her bed
She was playing a game on her Xbox at 11:58
It hit 11:59...
The power went out. The Wi-Fi went out...

Valeria walked out of her room and walked downstairs.
She saw her mum staring at a wall.
Her mum turned around revealing eyes black as a cat.
She ran at her.
Valeria ran out the door.
It was dead quiet outside.
Not a cat, not a dog, just nothing then she saw a black cat.
People told her black cats were bad luck but she thought they were good luck.

She petted the cat, it purred.
She then saw a monster.
It was black like coal then the cat disappeared so did Valeria.
She appeared in a black room.
The white cat was there.
Valeria was scared.
She had never been this scared before...

Layla Duthie (10)
Bellyeoman Primary School, Dunfermline

Nightmares

At night when you go to sleep at 10 to 11pm nightmares come out from everywhere, from closet to door and scares you. Only freedom is 6am. The monsters like darkness and fear light. You can't have dreams because they stop you having them. The monsters go to your mind and scare you. The only weapon is a flashlight to stop them from coming to your mind. Every hour they come to scare even more! As your mum shouts at you for not doing your homework and playing on your phone but nobody knows or believes...
At 2am the lights are turning on and off. Doors are opening and closing like a loop.
Nightmares are scary and huge. Crazy sharp teeth, eyes yellow like bright gold. All black. It can also make noises like bang and whizz. When it walks it's like someone is screaming in the floor.
Finally, the day is here, the sun will save me. But I won't be glad for long. The night will come again...

Zuzanna Gajda (11)
Bellyeoman Primary School, Dunfermline

A Dream Or A Nightmare?

I went to bed and thought of me decorating a gingerbread house,
Thinking I would dream of it.
Then I saw something...
It was a house-size gingerbread house.
I went inside and the door slammed behind me.
Bang!
I kept walking further and further,
Then suddenly the corridor came to an end.
I turned around and I got a fright,
It was a friend. My friend.
He didn't say anything but then I heard a creak,
It was like the floor was screaming.
My friend looked different though,
His eyes were bloodshot-red.
Then the ground started to shake.
My friend looked at me and said,
"Did someone make a smoothie?"
I looked at him strangely,
Then half of the house got bitten off
By my baby brother!
Oh boy, what will I tell my mother?

Molly Walker (11)
Bellyeoman Primary School, Dunfermline

Night Terror

As I lie in my bed
I think that I'm dead.
Witches surround me.
I wish I could be somewhere else,
Where I can hear the chiming of bells.

I wake up with a startled shriek,
I hear a door creak,
And a bang from under my bed.
Was this all in my head?
I am lying in my bed with monsters on my legs,
Suddenly I hear the cracking of eggs.

I am creeping down the stairs
When I get the scares.
Someone is behind me
I can't believe what I see!
A witch with a dress as black as the night sky
Suddenly the broom starts to fly.

I go back to bed
With muck on my head.
When I fall asleep again
The scary thoughts come to an end.
I have finally escaped this nasty scream
And now I can have a wonderful dream.

Olivia Rodrigues Teixeira (10)
Bellyeoman Primary School, Dunfermline

Once Upon A Nightmare

I was lying in my bed with a dizzy feeling in my head
I felt like I was dead, was it going to be the end?

In the shadows, something was creeping up,
It was a monster covered in muck.
Nightmares come and haunt your dreams,
Could I escape this terrible scream?
Was this all in my head?
They led me to a terrible place,
There was a horrified look on their face.

I woke up with a shriek and heard an awful creak.
Lying in my bed with monsters crawling up my legs.

Shadows were like monsters and they roared more and more.
The wind was tapping on my windowsill and then I heard this ghastly moan
But it was dark and cold and I felt alone.
Something happened, everything stopped.
I found a knife in my heart.

Jessica Cronin (11)
Bellyeoman Primary School, Dunfermline

Dream Land

Once you fall asleep images fill your head.
They feel so real but it's just your mind filling your head with dread.
I can show you how to get there.
It's very easy to find.
Lots of strange and magnificent creatures and objects as big as mountains and as small as mice.
Up the mountain you can hear them sing.
Why don't you take a ride on the flying dice,
What a crazy thing.

Then suddenly the mountains wobble like jelly.
Bang!
I have a bad feeling in my belly,
Then I see a strange creature with one big fang.
Then you wake up,
It's just a dream.
So this is the end because you woke up.
Next time it will be a different theme.

Oliver Platten (10)
Bellyeoman Primary School, Dunfermline

Once Upon A Dream

Once upon a dream
There was a mythical island with creatures.
You wouldn't even think of monkeys with wings and horns,
Dogs with rabbit ears and no fur like a hairless mole-rat.
The headmaster cut the sheep's wool as the sheep jumped in the pool.
There was a splash, swish and whoosh!

The dragon whooshed past the sheep in the pool.
"Wait!" said the headmaster.
He saw the sheep transform into a giraffe
Like how a chicken leg turns into a bone
Then suddenly the giraffe went against the headmaster.
The giraffe took the guy's clothes off
But then all along he was a kid!

Euan Simmonette (10)
Bellyeoman Primary School, Dunfermline

What It Is Like In My Dream World

In my dream world, it's sometimes a wee bit silly but it's simple and average there. Most of the time there is a football field with lion players vs tiger players. There's also an arcade. You can play for free on the machines if you like. There are also houses with video games, so much so that they're pixelated!
What's more in the arcade? you ask... A VIP lounge with a TV and a boxing arena!
The stage next to the arcade is better! There are flames that roar and dance, and the performers are as wild as crocodiles. Come and stay a bit, will ya? Cos I have a game for you to play.

Ram Leanillo (10)
Bellyeoman Primary School, Dunfermline

The Spooky Night

One mysterious night in a normal street it was a stormy evening.
Thunder and lightning struck.
A little boy called Jim could hear the stormy evening
And his bed did not feel right, it felt tight.
He woke up levitating by a nice witch.
She was helping him because he was abandoned.
She looked after him.
She had a cat called Tim,
He was very friendly.
He felt sad because he missed his mum and dad.
The witch's house had a caramel door and marshmallow windows.
The bricks were chocolate and the metal was lollipops.
The boy lived happily ever after.

Jackson Russell (10)
Bellyeoman Primary School, Dunfermline

What If...

What if...
That's one phrase I keep hearing a lot.
And I guess you do too.
For example, what if my house were made of swirly, lush, tasty, yummy chocolate?
Or my legs were replaced by whooshing rockets?
What if is not a question but a thing that is endless in infinity.
Tick-tock, tick-tock, that is the time.
Time can be an 'if' and some of the most confusing.
If it was the big bang or the dawn of the dinosaurs
Or even the far future.
For example yesterday the grass danced in the wind
Or my tummy was gurgling like a volcano today.

Conrad Abraham (12)
Bellyeoman Primary School, Dunfermline

Once Upon A Dream

In my dream land the land is dark
But lights shoot past like a bullet,
As fast as a big dog's best bark.
As the bullet of light flies past it thinks it will rule it.

In my dream land there are two big islands
One goes bang and the other one stays fine.
My rocket goes *whoosh* and goes to the moon
And then goes *boom!*
As it blows up again there is also a pool with a diving board that is pretty cool too.

There are aliens that fly around,
One is called Bob, he does a good job giving food to all.

Lewis Thompson (10)
Bellyeoman Primary School, Dunfermline

Once Upon A Time...

Once upon a time, a boy called Tyler woke up to a lion's roar in the thunder and lightning. Tyler looked out the window and he could not believe his eyes... He saw a portal to ancient Greece in the lightning and Zeus, Aries and the lion were surrounding him.
Then he looked to the other side and he saw Hades riding a three-headed dog through another portal going to war. Between them, Tyler saw Satan and Jesus fighting, also there were Minions fighting to the death.
In came an Olympic champion. Then in came God to wipe out all of the evil spirits.

Jay Brownlie (10)
Bellyeoman Primary School, Dunfermline

Deep Sleep

I woke up in my dream
As the night sky gleamed.
I saw a light shining bright
The stars shone when the night sky dawned.

The shadows danced,
The sunset pranced.

Red, pink, orange and yellow too,
All the colours of the sky soon to be dark blue.

As the butterfly whooshed past
I knew dreams don't last.
The grass crunched below my feet,
Sunflowers as tall as trees.

When I looked in front of me
I heard the birds say tweet, tweet
As I awoke from my sleep.

Alice Nicholson (10)
Bellyeoman Primary School, Dunfermline

A Deep Dark Dream

One night as I was lying in my bed
I thought of something that could make the world end.

Something cruel, something vicious,
Oh I know, a nightmare...

There so bold and real,
They could even maybe make you squeal!

Creak! went the floorboards so I turned around,
You'd be horrified if you saw what I found.

Nightmares come to haunt your dreams,
They say it's not real but how could that be true...

Because there's always someone watching you!

Ruby Popescu (10)
Bellyeoman Primary School, Dunfermline

Body Switch Up

Once upon a dream, I was sleeping in my bed peacefully but all of a sudden in my dream Natalie stormed into my room in tears. She was crying then she suddenly touched me and we were switching bodies. It was super weird and super wacky. When we were switching and twitching we were screaming then we went to the kitchen.

We were with our kitten who was sitting on the chair. I could hear the noisy air out there. It was making a noisy roar like a lion. I could see the bushes dancing with the air.

Neve Smith (11)
Bellyeoman Primary School, Dunfermline

Once Upon A Nightmare

Still awake, awake in the dark.
The clock hit 12:00.
I fall asleep.
Immediately knowing what would happen if I didn't...

The dream... In the pouring rain in trees,
Running, running from nothing, nobody, just running.
Am I dead? Is it going to be the end?

The rain splashing over me.
Running as the moon follows me.
I awake from an awful creak.
I wait until morning to tell my mum my awful dream!

Ella Reid (10)
Bellyeoman Primary School, Dunfermline

A Dream To A Nightmare

I was in a dream... A dream where there was a house, a great house. The house had blue bricks, yellow doors and it had lots of books. I loved it.
Then I looked around a bit and I ran into the basement. I looked in and I was scared to death. I ran up the stairs and I felt someone staring at me.
I ran out of that house, that crazy house! But then... I woke up screaming with fear. I think more danger was near!

Brogan Lamb (10)
Bellyeoman Primary School, Dunfermline

Cave Noises

To a large cave with deadly darkness,
A creature with huge white eyes and a monstrous smile stands high.

It's tall and slim
With a massive grin.
It's tall like a humungous tree,
I was fascinated more than I'd ever been before.

The large cave screamed.
As I walked in the cave I got a glimpse of the dweller of the cave,
It stomped then I woke up.

Isaac McKenzie (10)
Bellyeoman Primary School, Dunfermline

Super Boy

At the beach I saw a bracelet
I put it on...
Without warning I started to fly
Then a giant octopus came out of the water
It attacked me
But I couldn't defeat it
I was determined and my bracelet started to glow
I was filled with love
I filled the octopus with love
And made him feel happy
So he went back to the sea
Then peace came to me.

Leela Walker (9)
Bracoden School, Gamrie

The Flying Athlete

In the vast sky
A lone athlete soared with wings of strength
Their spirit roared
Through clouds and the sun, they flew with might
But lost their way in the fading light.

No map to show, no lane to see
They searched for home
Throughout the night
Through stars and wind
They travelled far
A flying athlete like a shooting star.

Logan McLean (10)
Bracoden School, Gamrie

Exploring Dragon Island

On my ship one day
I was heading to the bay
The ubiquitous pirates invaded
Soon I got kidnapped and I was in a bed
I got liberty and found a deserted island
There were dragons but soon I noticed it was in Thailand
They were magical and they could fly
Every day at 12pm they said goodbye!

Scott Ritchie (9)
Bracoden School, Gamrie

Once Upon A Planet

I slept like a baby but woke up like a rock.
It felt like I had fallen through planets,
And was in a pinball machine.

Why was it so loud and chaotic?
Planet to planet, man to man,
I got hit by a star like a frying pan.
I wish I could leave here in a snap,
Or fall through the planets and land on my back.

I tried to leave in a hurry,
But instead, ended up in a flurry.
Mars, oh Mars, why are you so red?
Calm down, don't lose your head!

Sun, oh sun, you shine like a knight,
Why are you so hot and bright?
Moon, oh moon, you look like cheese,
Can I have a little bite, please?
Earth is where I wish to be,
Wake me up and take me back there, please!

Freddie Folan (10)
Chigwell Primary Academy, Chigwell

My Dream About Money

Once upon a dream,
Something that seems way more than a dream,
Buildings as high as the sky,
Money's greener than trees
And everything is squeaky clean,
My mother would be pleased.
With people so posh, posher than me,
So effortlessly.

Looks like the future but way further in,
Money is like everything,
With elegance, it seems
People vrooming in cars so fast,
They might be able to travel back to the past.
People live in luxury but when they are hungry,
A fancy McDonald's is waiting on their bed.

Back to my dream...
Everyone is living like a king or queen,
Robots walking on the street, still fancier than me,
Children playing under the sun, having lots of fun.

Babies bathing in the sun all day long
Feels like the sun is smiling on us
Sunshine's here for everyone
Millionaires are spoken about like they're poor,
I wonder what they will call me...

Nelson Landing Flanagan (10)
Chigwell Primary Academy, Chigwell

Once Upon A Dream

One day, I woke up on a cloud,
Everything was still, nothing was loud.
I could see the blue gleaming sky from quite high.
The clouds felt like a soft pillow,
Every step I took, the clouds went *poof!*

Everything around me was silent like a mouse,
It was like the bright sun smiled at me.
Oh, how I wish this dream would never end.

I saw a small fragile cat,
With an ivory coat.
It whispered to me,
"This won't last forever."

When I blinked, everything disappeared,
I thought it was nothing, but it really wasn't.

I woke up and took a look around me,
I was home.
I guess dreams don't stay forever.

Humaira Islam (10)
Chigwell Primary Academy, Chigwell

Dreamland

In Dreamland, where everyone ponders,
Zooming in, let us take a closer look.
Apparently, Dreamland has cities,
Today, we are at Animal City.

Full of brilliant, bold beings.
Everyone is feeling over the moon.
Everyone has something to appreciate,
Jovial, gleeful, ecstatic.

Wolf, hawks, raccoons and jaguars,
Which all accompany me,
Creatures as talented as a dog,
Wondrous, dreamy, carefree.

Dozens and dozens and dozens of flowers,
All full of iridescent colours.
Whoosh, whoosh! exclaims the wind,
This place is amazingly adventurous.

Toluwanimi Adeyinka (9)
Chigwell Primary Academy, Chigwell

Once Upon A Dream...

Once upon a dream,
I saw a candy house,
A chocolate fountain and a big giant mountain,
Candyfloss clouds,
And river currants banging so loud.

As the majestic grass sways at my feet,
I feel like I need something to eat,
So I munch on all the sweets.
"Yum, yum," I said,
As the azure sky floats above my head,
In the distance, I see a bed.

As I get into the bed, I start to dream,
All about chocolate ice cream.
It looks really nice,
And this is where it comes to an end,
Bye-bye, dream world.

Olly Wymer (10)
Chigwell Primary Academy, Chigwell

When I Grow Up!

When I grow up,
I want to be a lawyer.
Lawyers make lots of money,
But some people think it's kind of funny.
I'm intelligent, responsible and fair,
But some people don't really seem to care.

I have many other dreams,
But this is the one I'm focusing on.
I dream so big,
Yet I am so small.

My parents want me to be a lawyer,
They are rooting for me,
They want me to make the money in the family,
I want them to be pleased for me,
As proud as anyone can be.

When I grow up...

Talia Gadiagellan (10)
Chigwell Primary Academy, Chigwell

Once Upon A Nightmare...

Once upon a nightmare,
In the distance,
There was a tiny cottage.
Don't go inside, for what you might see,
Will surely haunt your dreams!

Bang! The door slams behind you,
You shiver as you walk to the next room.
Drip... drip... drip...
Horrified and scared,
You wish you were dead!

Run, run, run,
Out of the house,
Running for my life.

Then, stop... I wake,
It was only a nightmare.

Nilisha Vimaleswaran (10)
Chigwell Primary Academy, Chigwell

Once Upon A Nightmare...

All I see are UFOs,
Like here and there, they go,
It is pitch-black in this hollow night,
It really is a fright!

I really need to wake up from this sleep,
Before I start to weep.
I really think I may never,
Wake up from this horrible terror!

Before I start to fade,
I must say bye to the UFOs that invade,
I am really starting to wake,
Finally, for goodness sake.

Lenny Wren
Chigwell Primary Academy, Chigwell

Nightmares

Nightmares come and go,
On a hollow night,
And give you a big fright!

They come in the dark,
And not in the light and day,
They don't come in a joyful way.

They will always come and go,
They will never stay,
They slowly fade away,

Unless you wake up with a scary face!

Shray Vekariya (10)
Chigwell Primary Academy, Chigwell

My Dream

Once upon a dream,
I was floating like a balloon.
In outer space,
Where the stars shone brightly.
As I flew past the planets,
The stars were winking at me.
I felt joyful and ecstatic,
Once upon a dream.

Clark Harman (11)
Chigwell Primary Academy, Chigwell

Zoe's Dinoland Dream

I always find it hard to get to sleep,
The only thing that helps is counting dinosaurs not sheep,
Every night I end up living in a crazy dream,
I just hope it makes me smile and not scream.

In my dreams dinosaurs roam around so grand,
In an awesome prehistoric dinoland,
The dinosaurs are all super cool,
They start the day with Frosties for breakfast before going to school.

T-rex wears a funny hat,
Stegosaurus loves to chat,
Triceratops does ballet moves,
Velociraptor jumps and grooves,
In dino school there is often a dance-off with the dino crew,
I just giggle and laugh, everybody does too.

In my dream, dinosaurs come to play,
Bright coloured, loud, they roam and sway,
I ride on the back of a friendly dino,
Through chocolate forests where rainbow rivers flow.

In my dreams the dinosaurs are big and strong,
But they are so gentle and my dino friends in Dinoland
are where we all belong.
So when I sleep and close my eyes tight,
I dream of dinosaurs with all my might.

Zoe Cartwright (9)
Larbert Village Primary School, Larbert

Talking Animals

There was a car in the night sky
There were bright colours flashing by
It could talk to you and fly,
Also, make a big poo just like a human
If you're a woman if you see an animal
It's more likely to be a mammal
It could talk and maybe also walk
The food they eat is mostly meat
The astronaut that can fit in a pot
You'll think you're awake but you're actually asleep
Falling right into a really deep dream
The astronaut that's in your dream
Is doing cartwheels along a beam
Talking to an animal that's driving cars across tall bars
Flying to the moon with several million baboons
Sleeping in lots of rooms
Having dreams in your dreams
Maybe also walking across beams
Night-night, sleep tight!

Sophia Ure (9)
Larbert Village Primary School, Larbert

The Wonderful World Of Dreams

Lights off, eyes shut tight,
Where will you go in your dreams tonight?
You could be living in a giant house
Or you could be a cat chasing a mouse.
You could be flying up to space
Or you could be a detective solving a case.
You could be a mermaid swimming in the deep, dark sea
Come on, let your imagination break free!
Dreams are really crazy, different for me and you,
You don't know what you'll see and you don't know what you'll do.
You don't always remember what happens in your dreams,
It's always really good but never what it seems.
You wake up in the morning, cosy in your bed,
But all of your dreams have disappeared from your head.

Jessica Thom (10)
Larbert Village Primary School, Larbert

My Magical Dog

One day, I was fast asleep. Suddenly the lights came on. I looked above my head and there was a dog. I loved it and shouted, "Yippee!" as happy as can be. I went on and on, talking till suddenly it spoke. I was as astonished as my mum getting fired so I played with it and played with it until one night it turned into a cat. I was scared because I am allergic to cats so I backed away and ran as fast as Usain Bolt. I easily escaped. But then it turned back into a dog. I didn't realise it was just my dog. So now we live a happy life in my luxury bedroom.

Oliver Smart (9)
Larbert Village Primary School, Larbert

The Light

Every night there is a light.
It tells me to follow it
But I'm not sure
It could lead me to a wonderful palace of dreams
Or a nightmare with demons that do bad deeds.
But one very night I decided to follow the light.
Oh my, what could I see?
A man jumping as high as a flea.
Dinosaurs and magical drawers.
Evil bees on their knees.
Then it was time to stop the rhyme.

I woke but I was in a lake.
I thought I was in a dream
But I was in real life.

Aaron Auchinvole (9)
Larbert Village Primary School, Larbert

It Must Have Been A Dream...

I was flying on my broomstick
Harry, Ron and Hermione had theirs too
We were flying around the school
Then we stopped because there was a pool
We jumped right in and looked around
But then there was a horrible sound
We jumped right out and flew back home
But we weren't looking and hit a pole
It just got more and more sore
Then I woke up and my head wasn't sore
Must have been a dream
That I didn't want anymore.

Sasha Wylie (9)
Larbert Village Primary School, Larbert

Flying Job

F lying through the night sky
L ying on the broom
Y ou don't believe me because you are not in the group
I n the black night you see me fly
N o, I don't lie
G lancing left and right

J umbling from broom to broom
O n one broom, time to go home
B edtime is now, it was all just a dream.

Emily Maclean (9)
Larbert Village Primary School, Larbert

Once Upon A Dream...

M y dreams are fun and exciting
Y ellow pebbles all around the big beach house

D aisies dancing in the back garden
R ed roses sitting on the grass
E merald-green water
A long line of birds sitting in a tree
M ajestic dolphins dancing in the water
S ea snails walking along the sea floor.

Katie Taylor (9)
Larbert Village Primary School, Larbert

Turtle Dino Legs

In my dreams at night
I see a dino who's not quite right
He has turtle legs and a gerry neck
And he doesn't know how to use any tech
He is as scary as a spider
So he is known as an outsider
If you see him in Jurassic Park
You must be as quiet as a mouse
Otherwise he'll tear you up
And blow you down like a straw house.

Lottie Wilson (9)
Larbert Village Primary School, Larbert

Water

In my dream I went through a portal
I saw a person, he was not a mortal.
This person was walking on water
And next to him I saw a small otter.
The water he was on, it was crystal blue
So clear you could see right through.
The otter jumped over his head
And then I woke up cosy in my bed.

Jasper Switzer (10)
Larbert Village Primary School, Larbert

Dream Job: Teacher

D rifting away in my bed
R eading pupils' stories,
E njoying them so much.
A dream has just come true,
M iss Lyon teaching a class.

J ust saying hi when I go in.
O pening my eyes to realise I am in my
B ed!

Ruby Lyon (10)
Larbert Village Primary School, Larbert

The Nightmare

In the day and in the night
In the dark and in the light
Spooky trees surrounding me
I forget reality
Running through an endless woods
Creepy clowns surrounding me
Smiling at me scarily
I don't know, is this the end?
Then I wake up safe in bed.

Ryan Wilson (9)
Larbert Village Primary School, Larbert

Taylor Swift

T he Story Of Us
A ll Too Well
Y ou Belong With Me
L over
O ur Song
R eady For It

S peak Now
W elcome To New York
I llicit Affairs
F olklore
T he Man.

Millie Nicolson (9)
Larbert Village Primary School, Larbert

Dragons

D eadly dragons are
R oaming the land
A ll dragons are big and scary
G iant and loud, small and hairy
"**O** h no," everyone screams, "we're
N ever going to live!"

Fraser Wallace (9)
Larbert Village Primary School, Larbert

Clowns

C lowns are scary and they like
L ollipops but
O nce they are born their mums say
"**W** ow, he's gonna be a menace
N o doubt about it!"
S o, overall they are not nice!

Leah Barrowman (9)
Larbert Village Primary School, Larbert

Gangsta Dogs

One night there were gangsta dogs
One dog felt bad so he helped a little kid
And then he became a leader
After that he risked his life and sadly died from it.

Connor Newlands (10)
Larbert Village Primary School, Larbert

A Flying Nightmare

Once I was flying in a big city,
Across a building.
I hit my head on the building.
I died but it was just a dream.

Ralph Walker (9)
Larbert Village Primary School, Larbert

Lava

L ight
A ctive
V olcano
A rt.

Murron Pettigrew (10)
Larbert Village Primary School, Larbert

My Dream Adventure

I woke up. I got dressed. I went outside but then I saw a massive black hole. Showing all my bravery I walked in. It showed a massive garden. The only thing was it had a door. I walked in. There were millions of buildings crumbled and thousands of superheroes and supervillains. I was terrified, I didn't know what to do. I was down there, screaming every second. I hated being there. I went to get out and I stood up. *So okay I'm ready,* I thought. I jumped from buildings. I felt unstoppable. I slipped. I felt I was going to die. At that moment I felt something. Some random superhero kicked me away but at that moment I noticed it was just me saving the world.
So my plan was to jump past holes until the villain fell and died but to my surprise it worked and everything was normal again. I heard screams of "Archie!" I woke up. It was my mum again. I jumped on my trampoline. I'm still here!

Archie Moore (9)
Lorne Primary School, Edinburgh

Apocalyptic World Of Zombies

One sunny day in the science lab, some scientists were working on a zombie cure but the power went out and the zombie escaped. It bit everyone and the infection spread. Survivors were running out of food. One of the survivors was Antonio who was good with a katana. It made shockwaves when it hit the ground so he could take the zombies down. And with his golden AK he was unstoppable.

Antonio was exploring and found a bigger and better refugee base with food. The guards would not let them in so he snuck in from the side and took some food. "Wow!" said Antonio. "They have a lot of food!" so he took all the food and left.

All the survivors were happy and were planning to flee on a boat but they could not find one no matter what and they couldn't walk around the city, it was massive so they went to every lake but found no boats. They tried to look for a car but they all had no gas. "The military base!" said Antonio.

"The military evacuated everyone on the aircraft carrier so their vehicles should have gas."

So they went into the base, got food and finally found civilisation and reunited with their families. But the military gave them an arrest warrant for using military vehicles so after a year in prison they were released.

Makarios Yerikema (9)
Lorne Primary School, Edinburgh

Zombie Park

There once was a boy called Allan and his friend, Archie. They decided to go to a scary place called Zombie Park which was recommended for zombies only. When they got there there were no zombies at all, instead there were goblins all around the park. Allan and Archie were scared until they noticed the goblins had invaded the park and not only the park because then they were going to invade the city!
Allan asked Archie if he had something to stop the goblins and the only thing he had was not very good, instead he only had a teddy bear and no of course that was not going to help so the goblins hit the boys with a hammer and they fell to the ground. The goblins made them drink a poisonous liquid and Allan was poisoned and nobody knows what happened to Archie. It was a mystery.

Allan Nuñez (9)
Lorne Primary School, Edinburgh

The Royal Kidnapper

One day I woke up to find myself in the kitchen. My sister, Helena, was telling me to wake up because I went to sleep very late. After seeing the time I got ready to go to the school party. It was so fun. When we went to sleep we saw the Northern Lights because I woke up to get water.

The next day we went to the park but Taleen noticed we were being followed so we ran as fast as the wind but they caught us. We got taken to a castle. We got put in a cellar. The person took their mask off and it was the queen. She had kidnapped us.

After five hours I found a bobby pin on the floor. It was Isabella's bobby pin so we put the bobby pin in the lock. We escaped. We went back home and locked all the doors. We went into the attic and hid under a blanket... Then I woke up!

Nora Salgado-Cerezo (9)
Lorne Primary School, Edinburgh

Lewis's Dream

One day I woke up in my bed. I got up and I realised it was a dream. I saw my mum in the living room. Me, my mum and my dad. We went out but as we did we got teleported somewhere. "Lots of doors," I said.
"Well let's go in one."
As we did I realised there were rooms for miles. We had hours of looking until we were outside. We went out and there was a silvery-looking dog. I was interested so I followed it and we ended up in a secret vault. There was lots of money, silver, gold, orbs and diamonds! I took everything and ran as fast as I could back into the house. I made a lot of money and I decided to get a dog and it was a silver one! I got people to build me a spaceship. After that, we were living normally and then I woke up in the house.

Lewis Burnett (9)
Lorne Primary School, Edinburgh

The Killer Clown

In the middle of the night there was a siren. I had chills down my spine. I looked out my window. I was shocked. I saw a killer clown! I ran downstairs and boarded my door. The killer clown was kicking my door, kicking it down fast. I ran upstairs. I looked at the door. The clown had a chainsaw. *I am gonna die tonight*, I thought.
I thought of an idea. I jumped out of my window. I ran away from my house. I hid somewhere. Later on the clown with a sword appeared. I went through the vent, got in a car and drove away. I went to get food. I found a police car. I found a flare and set it off.

Elliot Laidlaw (8)
Lorne Primary School, Edinburgh

The Creepy House

One day I went to a house and it was so dark and scary. I saw a monster eating Blaine! I fell and he saw me and he chased me to my house. I went to the basement. I stayed there for thirty minutes. The next day I was going to get him with my friends.
I was ready to get him with my friends. I was at the house. He wasn't there. We ran and we ran to the forest and we saw a man cutting a tree so we asked him to help us. The guy was chasing us and he said, "No way!"
We said, "Yes," and he believed us and he helped us. He took us to his house and he fed us.

Mason Tipton (9)
Lorne Primary School, Edinburgh

Magic Forest

I woke up and found myself in the forest but it was not an ordinary forest. Everything was glowing and it was very beautiful. There were a lot of plants, they were alive and a little scary. I made friends. It was very beautiful and fun. There were huge trees that glowed and I started living there. I taught my friends how to build mini houses for themselves. It was so nice. They built houses for themselves and then my mother woke me up and told me to get up and go to school.

Polina Kucher (9)
Lorne Primary School, Edinburgh

Castle Dream

I saw a castle. At night I went into the castle and I saw bones and some dead bodies. I saw dragons and snakes.
Someone said, "Why are you in my castle?"
I said, "Who are you?"
He said, "I am the Dragon Castle King."
I said, "Please don't kill me!"
But he killed me!

Afroze Faizan (9)
Lorne Primary School, Edinburgh

Living With My Friend, Helena

We played lots of games almost every day. We'd sleep together during the night. When we woke up the house was full of light. We played a game called 'Once Upon A Fright'. It was quite scary but not that much but then it was time for lunch. After lunch, we had pasta and played with the ball. It was so good!

Taleen Ujam (8)
Lorne Primary School, Edinburgh

I Don't Know

One time, on a foggy night
A witch came and said, "You get two choices,
You become a witch or a mermaid."
I said, "I don't know."
The witch cast a spell on me and said,
"You no longer have a choice.
You will become a witch!"

Cee Cee Mason (8)
Lorne Primary School, Edinburgh

The Hero

A magic fairy came to the hero, Billy. Billy didn't know he was a hero yet! The fairy gave him a magical sword and armour. Then the magic fairy sent him on a quest to kill monsters.

Akorede Agunbiade (8)
Lorne Primary School, Edinburgh

The Fortnite World Cup

World Cup...
A tough situation
We have the high ground
Bang! goes the heavy sniper
Just missed George but hit me 135hp
Top five situations Bugha and Clix,
Me, George and Mongal,
2am, wait! It's a two vs one
We tried to trickshot Mongal...

But wait, he spawned a dinosaur
We ran away but tried to fight back.
The dinosaur was as tall as a building
It clipped me but I lowered hp to 100
I died, it's just George.
He killed the dinosaur
George used the shock.
All I could see was George's POV.

One vs one,
George goes for the shockwave move
Hit him 199 he's one shot,
But he hits a shot.
George is at 17hp and Mongal is on top
Mongal hits George, 1hp both on top
Mongal is pushing George
But George shockwaves down
Hits the shockwave thunder pump and wins
We were stealthy and a ninja,
That is how we won, we were so happy
It was like a dream!

Rhys Rinaldi (11)
Netherthird Primary School, Cumnock

The Haunted House

I went to a scary haunted house
It was called the Loud House
There was a scary ghost walking around, *bang!*
The chair fell down
There were candles lighting up the wall
There was a window all smashed, *crash!*
If you go to bed you can hear screams and scares.

There was a scary creature in my bed
I was shouting, "Run, run!"
Slowly I went down the stairs.
The ghost was shouting, screaming with a loud dark voice
A chair was moving faster and faster
I went back up but the scary haunted creature was not there.

I was so scared,
The house had got flowers and grass on the wall.
Something shouted, "Run!"
Again I ran up the stairs and was so scared...
The creature was in my bed!

Khloe Carmichael (11)
Netherthird Primary School, Cumnock

Dream Land

In my dreams every night a dream land comes to life
In the glass-pink sky butterflies shine bright
Fairies and pixies are making poison
As I walk through the emerald floor
I come across poisons and pastries that make you grow tall
Those poisons and pastries make you fall.

The fairies dancing in the sky
The king fairy and queen pixie's palace
The dragon guarding the palace
The queen's dress is bright like crystals
The pixies giving out real crystals
Baby pixies crawling around.

Pixies singing to make me smile
Fairies making pastries for a while
As I dance away
I open my eyes
And I say, "That's enough excitement for one night,"
Then I go back to sleep.

Darcie Reid (10)
Netherthird Primary School, Cumnock

The Dream Goalie

In my dreams every night
Is a starry night sky
I always watch the saves be saved!
Even when the ball is as slippery as ice
She can still save amazingly.

She can save as fast as The Flash
She can come out big like The Hulk
And she is as good as a professional
She is at the top of her game
All her friends think she is amazing in goal.

She is a trap you can never get past
And she is like a door you can never slam
She is never slow to get the ball...
Then I wake up and realise it was all a dream!

Jorgie Hodge (11)
Netherthird Primary School, Cumnock

The Crazy Clown

Once upon a time
There was a crime
By a clown named Lime.
He packed his bags
So no one would know
Where he would go.

He pretended to be a dancer
He was a right chancer
He went to dance at the beach
But he saw something like a peach
The wind came
It sounded like a woman in pain.

The clown fell
Then he went to a door
And rang the doorbell
A person opened the door
"Do you have something to tell me?"

Caitlyn Williams (10)
Netherthird Primary School, Cumnock

Pirate's Life

A long, long time ago, a pirate sailed the seas looking for any type of treasure because he was a thief, a pirate! He sailed next to a monster! He tried to sail to the horizon but all he could get to was the death zone. He tried to sail, sail, sail away but he didn't realise his wonderful friends were cheering for him. He didn't hear it because of the roar! The monster was like a massive squid but with green and bubbly skin with around twenty yellow eyes staring at him. He sailed away from the monster but he turned back and, "Boo!" His friends scared him. He got sent into the water. He swam to the closest island, swimming from the boat, exploring the mystical blue ocean. Seeing the tropical fish, the colourful coral lighting up the ocean, filling up the sea with beauty. The fish swam, making bubbles and finally got back to the beautiful, golden, sandy island with clear water. He rushed to the tavern to get a drink and then went to his house to sleep.

Joshua Powrie (10)
St Sylvester's RC Primary School, Elgin

Dreams

Every dream is different
But it's as if mine are especially.
I feel as if I'm falling down an endless pit.
I wish they were as recognisable as a line.
But my dreams go up and down and up and round so I have no sense of time.
I wish I had dreams that showed how my life would be
Instead of being confused and not knowing what to do.
I wish that I could be free
From all of these confusing meanings.
I constantly feel like I'm falling asleep and waking up.
Why can't I just shut up?
If feels like I'm screaming
But really I'm just dreaming
Of a dream that won't happen.
I guess I should stop thinking so much about it.
Every dream I have is the same.

Blanca Mazela (11)
St Sylvester's RC Primary School, Elgin

Anything Can Happen

I n a world where the sky is always blue,
M any creatures think this is not true.
A world where anything can happen,
G oing from a unicorn to a flying dragon.
I n the sky there are dancing clouds bobbing up and down,
N ever do they stop looking like a clown.
A place where all animals are, just looking at the sun,
R eady to make a fast run.
Y ou probably think this is not true.

P robably even think this is a clue.
O pening to a new magical world
E ven a place where mystical creatures exist,
M any animals covered in mist.

All you have to do is imagine.
Nothing else.

Zofia Andrasovska (11)
St Sylvester's RC Primary School, Elgin

Once I Slept

Once I slept and woke up in a dream,
It was scary and gloomy,
The trees shook their hands!
I found a lot of bands then I ran out of the forest,
I was chased by hornets,
There was a park with chickens playing football.
They played on the hay.
There were roosters betting on who was better,
They cawed and clawed at the ball,
One had hit the wall
They played offside but one had hit his backside,
Some roosters rooted for the other team,
The match ended, I went to meet the players,
They all had layers of clothing on.

Alan Cetera (10)
St Sylvester's RC Primary School, Elgin

Once I Dreamt...

Once I dreamt of being a footballer
Scoring goals and becoming the best player.
Winning every match and trophy.
My parents being proud of my career
And I hope I'll be back here.
Home is where I'll be,
Playing for my home team and making them happy.
Once I dreamt of being a successful footballer
That makes the world cheer.

Bladean Blantier (12)
St Sylvester's RC Primary School, Elgin

Horses In The Clouds

In my happy dreams at night,
On the clouds with stars so bright,
Herds of horses flick shiny tails,
While they gallop along the clouds trails.

As I watch them perform their dance,
All around me they happily prance,
The leader kneels down on one leg,
"Get on my back," the horse does beg.

I lift my leg over his white shiny back,
Lots of hooves clap as I gallop on the track,
I leave carrots, hoping they will stay,
But they turn their backs and gallop away.

One by one clouds turned into my bed,
Then I knew this night was all in my head,
Although I was joyful its end brought me sorrow,
Maybe I will dream like this again tomorrow.

Alana Graham (11)
Thornton Primary School, Thornton

The Fight On An Island

T rees falling all around
H elping people build their homes
E normous dinosaurs eating people

F lying dragons in the air
I ncredible creatures to kill
G round shaking all the time
H eavy snow all around
T rees being planted

O ranges being thrown
N ever-ending battles

A ngry people swimming away
N o one is safe

I ce all over the lake
S creaming children run for their lives
L ong-necked brachiosaurus eating trees
A bandoned buildings all over
N oisy dragons roar out loud
D inosaurs and dragons in my nightmares.

Charlie M (11)
Thornton Primary School, Thornton

The Magical Pen

In my dreams was a girl called Evie
Who lived with her big brother, Stevie
They found a book
And a pen with a hook
And drew a cute dog called Phoebe.

But suddenly to their surprise
Their cool drawing came alive
They jumped up and down
Danced all around
Feeling so happy they high-fived.

So they started drawing more
Like rainbows and delicious s'mores
Romantic roses
Flamingoes doing poses
Until they heard a big roar!

So in a rush, off they fled
Suddenly I woke up in dread
Sweat ran down my cheek
I felt a bit weak
So I decided to stay in my bed.

Grace Muldoon (10)
Thornton Primary School, Thornton

Portal In The Park

In my dreams I go to the park
I see a portal in the dark
It draws me close and I go through
A gerbil welcomes me with a moo.

A monkey swings down from a tree
He neighs then gives me a secret key
It takes me through a special gate
Oh what is happening? I cannot wait!

We enter a world of clouds and sky
And see an elephant flying high
We go to the sunny land below
And find a unicorn in the snow.

I love it here, I wish I could stay
But I'll have to rise at the start of day
In my future dreams I hope I can return again
To this magical land.

Lucy B (10)
Thornton Primary School, Thornton

Jurassic World

J ungle? I'm in a jungle.
U nbelievably I see a dinosaur.
"**R** un! It's trying to eat us!"
A nd Charlie, Grace, Summer and I
S tart seeing more dinosaurs.
S uddenly Charlie trips
I nto a swamp.
C an we save her?

W e help her and run away.
O n a tree Grace says, "We need to escape!"
R ustling leaves mean a dinosaur is near.
L uckily I wake up in my bed.
D on't want to go back there again!

Kerensa T-S (10)
Thornton Primary School, Thornton

Flying Animals

F ast asleep in my bed
L ooking at the bright blue sky
Y ellow snakes fly through the air
I wonder where I am
N ewts fly from tree to tree
G iraffes have wings of blue

A nimals are soaring everywhere
N ever seen anything like it
I love this wonderful strange world
M onkeys flit around my head
A kangaroo lands on my shoulder
L ittle gerbils flap and flutter
S oon I wake up and remember my magical dream.

Brianna T (11)
Thornton Primary School, Thornton

The Runaway Nugget

Once there was a nugget named Jack
Who had a very large back
He would run away
To get his own way
And put all his stuff in a sack.

He went away on a train
And he was in loads of pain
But to his surprise
A dog caught his eye
And he felt much better again.

Then Jack decided to leave home
And travel onward to Rome
He saw Inter Milan
It was all going to plan
Then he woke up and did his hair with a comb!

Jack P (10)
Thornton Primary School, Thornton

The Boy Who Turned Wolf

N ight-time came and I fell asleep
I woke up in deep, dark woods
G rey clouds and a full moon were in the sky
H owever I felt strange
T eeth to fangs, fur sprouted, nails to claws and clothes ripped
M y body transformed into a wolf
A light fog surrounded me
R eally terrified animals ran and hid
E erily, now I am a werewolf.

Adam H (11)
Thornton Primary School, Thornton

The Comic Dimension

I gently drift off to sleep
And see a changing coloured sky
My dogs are close by my side
To my surprise SpongeBob says, "Hi!"

My dogs start to talk
What is going on?
There's a cartoon city all around
Are we in ComiCon?

Oh no, I can see The Joker
He is giving a warning
I feel so scared and frightened
Oh thank goodness it's morning!

Casey M (10)
Thornton Primary School, Thornton

Football

F ootball is in my dreams every night
O n the football pitch I score and everyone is chanting
O n the touch I shout at the striker
T he striker passes to me and I shoot and I score
B lack and white ball on the ground
A fter the match everyone is shouting my name
L ooking around enjoying the atmosphere
L aughter and fun after the game.

Mitchell A (11)
Thornton Primary School, Thornton

The Space Train

On a train
In the rain
Excitement came
On the train

Through the clouds we race
Shock on my face
As we pick up pace
Travelling in space

Around the stars
We visit Mars
We travel afar
It's so bizarre.

The time I did spend
Was fun with my friends
But now we descend
My dream's at an end.

Dexter M (10)
Thornton Primary School, Thornton

The Strange World

I woke up in a world
Not so different from yours
Where the sun brightly shone
And humans were not known.

There was no land in sight
And the sky was white
And where there was always light.

But then it turned night
And I got a massive fright
As back came the light
As my mother spoke and I awoke.

Freddie Fox (10)
Thornton Primary School, Thornton

Blue Bears

B ig big bears in space
L ovely bear dreams
U nbelievable sights to see
E verywhere I go I see cute bears

B lue bears dancing
E very bear is colourful
A mazing stars in the Milky Way
R ude bears make fun of the blue bear
S mall bears making fruit smoothies.

Caitlyn B (11)
Thornton Primary School, Thornton

Bee And Me

I wake up in my bed
I hear a noise that fills me with dread
As I take a step out of the room
I see a giant bee that likes to roam
As I get hunted by the giant bee
I wonder why it has to be me?
As I get stung, I figure out
It is just a dream!

Tyler T (10)
Thornton Primary School, Thornton

Flying Dog And Dinosaur

In my dream at night
I saw an incredible sight
I was by a castle great
With my dinosaur and dog called Nate.

Then we flew up to the moon
We got there in a zoom
There we went to a fairy school
We really felt extremely cool.

Poppy Donaldson (11)
Thornton Primary School, Thornton

A World Inside My Head

The world inside my head,
No guards it has.
Where mountains climb the sky so high,
Birds soar from peak to peak,
The only rule is to challenge your limits,
Never limit your challenges.
But beware, turn it upside down
And you'll get the place where nightmares are born.
Where evil wizards with tall pointy hats
Wait in the shadows.
Dragons wait in their caves.
Bloodthirsty creatures,
Just dripping, waiting for more,
With dead black scales,
Fangs like daggers
And red eyes that glow in the fire.
But come back to Dream World
And find the biggest fluffiest cotton candy clouds
And cross the candyfloss river
And into the candyfloss forest

Into the clearing where the forest gives way
To a cottage that is made of toffee bricks
And strawberry laces for a roof
And inside you will find your happily ever after.

Jenna Spy (10)
West Coats Primary School, Cambuslang

Dreams And Nightmares

Here in Dreamland, you can have the time of your life,
That is until the nightmares come.
From puppy dreams to sad dreams,
From mummy dreams to dad dreams
There's always got to be a nightmare or two.
When you're dreaming of lots of fame,
There's got to be a nightmare.
Sometimes of monsters, sometimes of spiders.
There's always a nightmare.
Dreaming of Spider-Man,
Fred is asleep, until he has a nightmare,
Of course he has to weep.
Alice was having so much fun in her dream until...
"Mum!"
Creepy clowns were trying to trap her
Until she saw a familiar figure,
It was Wonder Woman, her favourite hero.
Five minutes later she was with Leo, her best friend.
But her dreams had come to an end.
She was just getting ready for school
But couldn't stop thinking about how dreams rule.

Arran Forbes (9)
West Coats Primary School, Cambuslang

Hades' Horses

Hades was an evil man. He was all blue. His skin was blue and his hair was blue flames. Hades was preparing and practising for his race. He had three horses named Nightmare, Skelly and Ritual. Their eyes were emerald-green and shimmery like the moon at night. Their coats were glazing like the sun shining on the river. Their hooves were sparkling like glitter. When they were doing the race they were sprinting like cheetahs. There were only two minutes left of the race and Hades was in third place. He had had enough. Hades decided to get the sharp blades out of his carriage. Hades cut Zeus' carriage wheels. Zeus' horses got insecure and ran away. Zeus was then disqualified. Hades was now in second place. He was right beside Hercules. Hades did the same thing to get Hercules disqualified. Hades won the race, unfortunately.

Isla Fraser (10)
West Coats Primary School, Cambuslang

The Girl Who Did What She Should

She never misunderstood.
The girl tapped and sang,
Her whole world was in her hand.
She went on a hike with her brother, Mike.
She got lost and got a fright,
Luckily she had enough food for the night.
She saw a cave not far away
So she celebrated and said, "Hooray!"
She sat down for the night
As the stars twinkled in the light.
She felt a rock move and it was not smooth,
It had scales, each one as big as sails!
She looked back to see a big blue eye as big as the sea,
She saw bones on the floor,
Her jaw dropped to the floor.
She thought it was a dream.
She felt shivers up her spine!
Boom, crash, splat!
She just woke up from a cold dream.

Julia Laing (9)
West Coats Primary School, Cambuslang

The Little Famous Actress

I dreamt of myself when I was older. An actress. All I wanted to do was go on a TV show and spread the joy. But here's the thing, none of my friends believed that I would grow to be successful so I wanted to prove them wrong.
Boom!
Twenty years later I succeeded. I proved my friends and family wrong.
I grew up. I made loads of money and I became an actress. I went on millions of TV shows and made my own make-up brand. But I found out that a friend from all those years ago signed up for my role! This was bad news but I knew what to do.
I met up with her, had lunch and said, "Please give me this role, I have always wanted to do it!"
She agreed but it's years later she still hates me.

Eva McNab (9)
West Coats Primary School, Cambuslang

Fantasy Hoppers

I got teleported into space
There was this guy coming at me at an alarming pace
He said, "Hi this is Dorgstool."
"Wow! This place is very cool.
He said, "Let's go to this grassy island next,
But let me just get this fixed... Anyways"
"Look at this bug, it is as green as an emerald
And as shiny as a diamond."
"Yes, yes that's a dorny bug."
"That's weird, it rhymes because it's on a thorny rug."
"Let's go to this flame island now."
"Cool!"
"I see a flame cow."
"Look, a dragon,
Wait...
The teleporter can begin."

Callum Forrest (9)
West Coats Primary School, Cambuslang

The Pit Of Doom

It was late at night, no clouds in the sky.
I heard a big pop, the lights went off.
I went to sleep, there was a bang.
It sounded like a mirror.
I saw it there was a pit.
Bottomless darkness, no light to be seen.
Until a man, about ten foot, pushed me into the pit.
I felt I was falling for eternity until out of the corner of my eye there was light.
A faint house.
It fell out of sight, I was terrified, petrified
Until my mum woke me up,
Or so I thought...
I woke up in the crusty house,
It was dusty.
Someone touched me from behind.
It was a clown.
I woke up in the night while the stars were sparkling in the night.

Callum MacLeod (9)
West Coats Primary School, Cambuslang

Magical Meteorite

Magical meteorite in the sky
Your light is so bright
Your glory makes stars sad
As you shoot across the sky
You immediately catch my eye
I follow you up the hill
Suddenly I'm standing still
Looking up at the sky, smiling at you
You smile back before you wreak terror
Killing my mother and my father
He walks up the road wrapped in fire
We bow down to him in fear and terror
I'm scared out of my socks so I stand up
And say, "Who asked you?" with a quiver
Then I walk away...
Magical meteorite in the sky
Grant my wish or I shall die
Grant my wish if you please
Now I must leave.

Grace Shields (9)
West Coats Primary School, Cambuslang

Lord Of The Rings: Fellowship Of The Ring

Once upon a time, in a mythical world there was a war.
Twenty thousand years ago, it was carnage.
Arrows, bombs, fireballs, spears, everything.
It was bonkers but one soldier changed it all.
George, your average knight had planned it all.
He would sneak to the dark lord and slay him.
And to save his baby.
He wanted to return the world to the way it was.
He then snuck in Mt Rage to see the dark lord.
George snuck up and struck the dark lord.
Ending his soul, then he picked up the ring,
And threw it in the flames of Mt Rage.
Ending the war and saving the world.

Logan Thomas (10)
West Coats Primary School, Cambuslang

Barbie Girl

How Barbie... How is your hair so perfect?
Your hips so slim?
Your teeth so white?
I wish I could be like you.

How Barbie... How do you have friends coming from left and right?
I wish I could be like you.

How Barbie... How are your legs so perfect?
Your outfits so prim?
You're perfect like pink icing on a cake.
I wish I could be like you.

Do I need to be perfect?
Barbie, your attitude is so rude.
I'm not like that.
I might not have your looks but at least I'm pretty on the inside.
I don't need you, Barbie.

Erin Carr (10)
West Coats Primary School, Cambuslang

Into The Lake

I was dropped into a deep, dark place
With no light and not much space.
A small island in the middle of a lake.
Gurgling water swimming with strange figures and shapes.
One quiet room with a singular sound.
I swam and swam away from the monsters.
With a splash, a splash and a splotter
I reached for a wooden ladder.
When I breached the ladder I started to climb
With a bumble, a stumble and quite a few mumbles I reached the top.
And to my surprise, it was my P4 class with their tiny little eyes.
I was sent to my seat as I was quite late.

Lucy Woodcraft (9)
West Coats Primary School, Cambuslang

My Brother Flying In The Sky

In my dreams, every night, my brother and I went to this house that had sweets on the door. The door was not shut. When we went inside the door shut then the wind howled in the night. Then someone whispered, "Go outside!"
My brother said, "No!"
Then I said, "Yes!"
My brother said, "Okay!"
Then we walked outside.
My brother said, "I don't feel well," then something happened. My brother started to fly in the sky but I didn't know what happened. He started floating higher and higher then he disappeared!

Mia Chow (10)
West Coats Primary School, Cambuslang

World Of Football

F un, enjoyable game. Football is my life!
O n the football field there are experienced and confident players.
O ne day I had a dream of scoring in a game.
T oday is the most important game of my career, scoring was my dream.
B ut first half 3-0 down, but second half I was ready.
A fter the game of hard work the final score was 5-4 to us.
L ater on I went to training. We learned that we had to play the best team in the league.
L ater the game finished. Blood, sweat and tears of joy and sadness.

Scott Allen (9)
West Coats Primary School, Cambuslang

The Dream That Changed My Life

What do I want to do with my life?
What do I want to do with my life?

I got sucked into a portal.
What do I do?
I heard a *pop, creak, crash, zoom!*
I don't yet know and I feel like my head is going to blow.
Now in my dream I have seen all these different jobs
And I still don't yet know what I want to do.
I feel torn and sore.
Defeated and more.
But I think I found what nobody yet knows…
I hope that some people believe in me
And I finally know.

Millie Glover (9)
West Coats Primary School, Cambuslang

The Killer Penguins Rule The World

Lots and lots of stacks but one of them was shaking a lot. All of a sudden an emperor penguin jumped out of a stack of dead people. I rushed upstairs to get to safety then slammed the door shut and locked it. Then they broke a hole in the wall so they could try and kill me. By now I was running for my life, jumping and running over penguins. Then I got to the town hall and shouted in the intercom, "Everyone, penguins are ruling the world!" And that was the last speech I ever made because the penguins murdered me!

Finn Scott (10)
West Coats Primary School, Cambuslang

In My World

In my world crocodiles drive cars
And humans can travel all the way to Mars.

Candyfloss clouds make a haze of pink
And to order food all you do is think.

Gluggers (a friendly type of alien) speak blob
And come from the planet of Malain!

"Bloby bloo bla!" they say with a smile.
But they hurt me when they're sad, it goes on for a mile!

That's my world, where tigers go blup,
But sadly, now the beep and smell of pancakes wakes me up!

Orla Dyer (10)
West Coats Primary School, Cambuslang

The Portal

I'm playing with my brother
He climbs the bunk bed
I look to my left
I see a big hole
Where is he now?
I guess I have to find out
I fall into the hole
It's rainbow with sweets everywhere
I see him running to the cake
Eating the sweets
I don't want him to get a sugar rush
He is running away from me
Taking all of the lollipops and sweets
What do I do now?
I see him eating a strawberry.
We enjoyed ourselves!

Shanzay Zahid (10)
West Coats Primary School, Cambuslang

Moving Monsters

I was at a disco dancing as normal,
Then people walked in, not looking so formal.

They were monsters that came out of nowhere,
The first one to dance was as green as a pear.

They took up the entire disco floor.
Then I realised there was more,
How is there more? I wonder.
And the next song to come on was 'Thunder'.

I was about to start busting moves.
But I busted something else...
My alarm clock!

Cooper Scott (9)
West Coats Primary School, Cambuslang

The Trip To Hell

Someone is watching me.
And I have a broken knee.
I can't really run
And I have a bun.
The sky is as clear as the sea
I see a forest, it's not that far.
But I see a foe as well
And my friends are scared
And none of them dared to go in
But I was brave enough to go in.
My friends followed and lightning danced across the sky
And the leaves waved in the wind
And there was a pop and a whizz!

Aaron Cole (9)
West Coats Primary School, Cambuslang

A Glitch In Reality

I wake up in a dream.
It seems all peaceful, right?
Until the clock strikes midnight.
I get a fright,
Everything turns pitch black,
Like as dark as the night sky,
Then four more weird and wacky tornadoes spin around at dashing speeds.
Everything that the tornado touches turns pixely!
I woke up.
The first thing I saw was a glitch in reality.

Theo Nicolson (9)
West Coats Primary School, Cambuslang

Footballers

F amous footballers
O nside
O ffside
T ierney
B enzema
A lisson
L ionel Messi
L úcio
E ndo
R onaldinho
S coring goals is what I like.

Daniel Butler (9)
West Coats Primary School, Cambuslang

Imagination

I t truly is a wonderful thing, all the laughs it will bring
M agical ideas filling your head
A t night-time when you're in your bed
G orgeous animals, people too
I nto a world all about you
N ever-ending happiness all around
A ll of the forgotten suddenly found
T ake a look at all of the smiles
I t reaches out for miles and miles
O n a train or on a bus
N ow, that's a secret just for us.

No one can live without imagination
It doesn't take any concentration
Once the thought is in your mind
You can create anything mean or kind.

Mabel Edwards (9)
Willoughby Primary School, Loughborough

Gymnastics

I arrive at the sports hall where I dream to be
The greatest gymnast for everyone to see
I swing on bars and dance on the beam
Everyone's impressed with my new routine
As I twist and turn, the crowd holds their breath
I love to perform, the feeling's the best
I look to the judges, they score me a ten
I can't wait to do it all over again.

Rae Tattersall (7)
Willoughby Primary School, Loughborough

Dream

D ay and night there can be dreams
R ight there in your mind
E ven though they may look fake, they're as real as can be
A ppearing in your mind like a program on the screen
M ighty strange they can seem as you gently lift your head.

Jessica White (10)
Willoughby Primary School, Loughborough

Monster

Running around you, watching your every move
It's with you on the full moon
As scary as a clown, as venomous as snake
It pounces... then you are awake.

Isabelle Cook (9)
Willoughby Primary School, Loughborough

YOUNG WRITERS INFORMATION

We hope you have enjoyed reading this book – and that you will continue to in the coming years.

If you're a young writer who enjoys reading and creative writing, or the parent of an enthusiastic poet or story writer, do visit our website **www.youngwriters.co.uk**. Here you will find free competitions, workshops and games, as well as recommended reads, a poetry glossary and our blog.

If you would like to order further copies of this book, or any of our other titles, then please give us a call or visit **www.youngwriters.co.uk**.

Young Writers
Remus House
Coltsfoot Drive
Peterborough
PE2 9BF
(01733) 890066
info@youngwriters.co.uk

YoungWritersUK   **YoungWritersCW**
youngwriterscw   **youngwriterscw**